He Hits!

HOPE for
battered women

And I will restore to you
the years that the locust hath eaten,
the cankerworm, and the palmerworm,
my great army
which I sent among you.
Joel 2:25 (KJV)

He Hits!

HOPE for battered women

by
Janet Jonathon

lifting up the Light of the world

Star Books Inc.

Wilson NC 27893

Library of Congress Cataloging in Publication Data:

Jonathon, Janet.
        He hits! Hope for battered women.

        Bibliography: p.
        1. Abused wives--Religious life. 2. Jonathon, Janet.
3. Abused wives--Biography. I. Title.
BV4596.A2J66 1989   248.8'435   89-4507
ISBN 0-91541-44-0

Published by
Star Books, Inc.
408 Pearson Street
Wilson, NC 27893

Telephone (919) 237-1591

ISBN: 0-915541-44-0

TABLE OF CONTENTS

to Karen,
my David-friend
who was a special, healing instrument
of God's love to me.
If I can minister to just one person
as you have ministered to me--
it will all have been worthwhile.

Prologue

Why would I want to write another book about battered women? I have asked myself. There are so many. But then I took another look at those books only to find that almost all were written by counselors and not by the women themselves. I guess that is my answer.

For fifteen years, I lived with the reality of an abusive spouse. I went through these experiences, I felt them, and I can share with you how God is restoring me.

For that reason, I feel that my poems can convey a depth of feeling and add a dimension that the other books lack. Not that the other books are bad. They are excellent, and I learned a lot from each one. At the end of my story, I have included a list of the books that were the most helpful to me.

But the most important reason for writing this is my desire to help other women in similar circumstances--to provide hope even in the most hopeless of situations. *God can restore!*

It is my hope, too, that men will read my book. Maybe it will enable them to recognize the pressure points in their own marriages, to give them hope that God can restore *everything*--even the damage done by battering cycles in troubled marriages.

The details of my story are true. Peoples' names have been altered to protect their privacy.

I would like to acknowledge my thankfulness to the people in my life who helped read and edit this book. I learned much from each one. They not only helped with the book, they helped with my healing. Special thanks to Karen, Bernadine, and Brad, who gave so much of their time and love to me.

Chapter 1

Marriage

Part 1

My Goal: Marriage

I wanted to be married.
I was 22,
and I thought I had found a man who loved me.
I wanted to be a wife and mother.
I thought marriage
was the most important goal of life--
more important than
my own personal goals and growth.

Our backgrounds were so different
but I naively assumed
that love would conquer all.

Tim and I took a marriage course together in college.
How strange that I don't remember anything significant
about that course.
I only know it didn't include any chapters
about violence,
and police,
and lawyers,
and restraining orders.

Who would have thought I needed to know
these things?
. . . I just wanted to get married!

He Hits!

A Bar Scene

"The books" say that before
a woman enters
into an abusive relationship,
she sees *a sign*--
at least one sign--
of what is to come.
This was my sign:

When we were dating,
I thought Tim was kind.
He seemed quiet
and laid back.
I saw him angry
only one time.

We were in a bar.
He wanted to go somewhere else
and I did not.
He slapped me across the face.

I was totally shocked.
No one had ever slapped my face before!
I remember thinking that if I had an engagement ring,
I would have taken pleasure in throwing it back at him.

But my parents were in the middle of wedding plans,
so I convinced myself that
this was an isolated incident.
I denied my feelings.
An isolated incident . . .

I was wrong;
he wasn't kind.

Hope for Battered Women

In the Womb

"My baby!"
I screamed inside my head.
"You're going to hurt my baby!"

I backed into the kitchen sink
away from the force of Tim's kicks
into my stomach.
My hands moved protectively,
to cover the tiny life within me.
I dodged away and fled to my neighbor's house,
only to find I couldn't tell her what was wrong,
once I got there.
Inside my head,
I was still screaming,
"My baby!
My baby!
You're going to hurt my baby!"

Humiliation

The force of the water surprises me
as it flies out of the glass in Tim's hand.
It drips off my face and clothes
as I try to deal with yet another humiliation--
another instance of his anger--
another attempt to control me.
And, oh, he can control me,
as I cower from his rage.

I try to comfort my small son as he becomes aware
of the confusion and tension all around him--
as Andy watches the water
slowly
drip
off
my
face.

Vulgar Language

I've always hated bad language--
gross, obscene words.
When I was growing up,
my world was much more sheltered.
I never heard more than "damn" at home,
and even that was rather rare.

Suddenly
I was faced with marriage
and anger words.
He used disgusting, degrading, put-down words,
alternated with "Honey,"
when he wasn't even mad.
This made me feel like a yo-yo--
whirled back and forth between the two extremes.
Tim never used my name.
I felt like just "a thing."
And his not-so-subtle
expressions of "so called" humor
were so demeaning to me as a woman.

Vulgar language--
a form of abuse all its own.

The Hospital Cover-Up

I love dancing
but can never interest Tim.
Today is Friday, and while we're building our house,
Tim decides that we will go out
to dinner and dancing.
I am looking forward to it so much!
       But now, after dinner, I'm exhausted.
       Already today,
       I've gotten up at five o'clock,
       taken care of our two small children,
       fixed three meals,
       and helped pour and trowel
       many yards of wet cement.
Back inside our house,
Tim is so mad
because I don't want to accept his sacrifice.
He hits me hard in the shoulders.
I can't believe the injustice of the situation
and instead of crying, like I usually do,
I get mad too. I hit him back!
That isn't very smart.
He goes for my face.
And as I put my hand up to shield my nose,
the blow from his fist breaks my finger.
Now he has to drive me to the hospital.
X-rays.
Questions.
I'm almost hysterical,
but I lie to cover up for him.
I am too ashamed to admit that he has hit me.
Anyway, he's standing right beside me.
I lie,
but I keep wondering if they know . . .

Isolated

Isolated--
I feel so isolated.
I live alone on twenty acres
of trees and mountainsides
and I can't even see
my neighbors.
Living here is
a compromise
between where he wants to live--
on 3,000 acres
in the middle of
Montana or Alaska--
and where I want to live--
in the middle of a neighborhood
with people to talk to
and playmates for my children.
Somehow I feel like
I still lost.
My friends don't
just drop in
and the children and I
are alone
almost every day.
I have no support system
and no family close by.
Compromise . . .
Sometimes I feel like
I still lost.
I
feel
isolated!

He Hits!

I'm Canning as Fast as I Can!

How I hate canning!
I've been in this kitchen since early June.
The days count by in jars--not weeks--
strawberries, cherries, apricots,
green beans, peas, corn,
grape juice, peaches, pears.
And now it is September and I'm still here . . .
slaving away.
Just one more jar of applesauce to fill,
so I can reach my 400-jar quota for the year.
I'm so tired,
so hot,
surrounded by steaming kettles,
and mounds of fresh vegetables from the garden
until I want to scream!
My children are fretful
and bored.
I want to play with them,
to take them to the park
or to the swimming pool.
They'll grow up so fast!
And will they remember that I couldn't
ever play with them?
I'm feeding their growing bodies
but I know inside myself
that I'm starving their little souls.

Inside this jar
drips applesauce
and tears.

Hope for Battered Women

A Professional Woman

I was a professional woman
when Tim met me.
Busy at college,
preparing to graduate,
working a part-time job,
editing my college yearbook.
He must have been attracted to
that kind of a woman.

Yet after we were married
he seemed determined to change me,
to mold me
into a farm wife
like his mother.
Stay at home,
bake bread,
make pies,
can food.
Stay at home, don't use gas,
never leave the farm . . .
"Barefoot and pregnant!"
My soul cries out,
"I am a professional woman! "
But professional women
can be victims too!

He Hits!

The Stereotype of Abuse

It just kills me:
everyone seems to think
that abuse happens only
to a certain
"stereotype"
or class of people--
people of poverty,
or of low education.
I mention abuse
and people seem to see
a woman with a black eye
working on the assembly line . . .
and they can't envision *me.*
To limit dysfunction to one category of people
is really the biggest lie--
I don't fit those prescribed roles.
I'm wearing designer clothes
on the outside
but I feel like
value-village
on the inside.
How did Tim sense
my lack of self-esteem?
Now he continues to add to
those feelings of inadequacy:
"You're so stupid, can't you do anything right?"
How can I believe his lies?
But
I
do . . .
believe his lies,
I'm *living* his lie.

The Emotional Temperature-Taker

I am always the emotional temperature-taker.
Will he come home upset tonight?
Will he be mad?
Maybe if I do
everything
just right,
things will be smooth.
Maybe if I could just learn
to be perfect,
I could prevent those outbursts of anger
directed at me.
It must be me,
mustn't it?
I pace the floor,
I wring my hands,
marking off the checklist in my head.
Is dinner ready?
The house picked up?
All the closet and cupboard doors shut?
Is the heat up too high?
Lights left on in any room?
Whew! Everything is done!
But as I hear his car driving up the gravel driveway,
I hear the phone ringing.
O God! I can't be talking on the phone
when he comes in . . .
O God

I Keep Silent

I keep silent.
I've lived with his anger,
with abuse,
so long . . .
and I bury the pain inside,
deep inside.
I am ashamed.
Sometimes
I go days without
even thinking about it.
And I don't get angry,
I'm just depressed.
Sometimes I want to talk,
to share,
but no words come out.
I've kept my inner silence so long,
it has become
an outer silence too.
If I say,
"Help me! My husband is abusing me,"
people might say,
"Well, what are you going to do about it?"
and I don't know,
I'm not ready . . .
. . . I keep silent.

Bruised!

Bruised!
You made the excuse
that you were
out of control,
but I don't think it's that way at all.
I think your abuse
is *very* controlled.
You always carefully choose--
the place
(where I am alone)
the time
(when the children are in bed)
and the part of my body that won't show.
Oh, yes, I was bruised--
so bruised that sometimes it hurt
even to have a hug from a friend--
but no one saw,
no one knew.

Things!

"Things"--
whoever said I wanted "things"?
You worked and worked
and said that you were doing it "for me,"
when all I wanted
was companionship
and love.
I followed you around
like a puppy dog,
trying to talk with you
while you hammered, weeded, welded, sawed.
You couldn't hear me
above the noise of those machines
(or your thoughts).
So eventually I gave up talking . . .
and you just kept on working.

Did you even notice I was gone?
Maybe for you,
work was a substitute
for love.

"Things"--
whoever said I wanted "things"?

Money

Money seems like a god
to Tim.
He controls it.
I brought it to the marriage
but he controls it.
He is so obsessed with saving,
with investing
where and when he wants to,
that money isn't even in the checkbook.
He is making a good salary,
but sometimes I can't
even buy
shoes for the children.
He doesn't value me
or my contribution to our family.
His salary should be my money too!

Oh, yes,
he asks my opinion:
"Honey, shall we invest in this?"
but he only wants to hear my "yes."
So, of course, I say "yes," but I'm thinking--
You've got to be kidding!
Thirteen thousand dollars
in one oilwell?
And then he ridicules
even my smallest financial decisions:
"How can you spend twelve dollars
for one haircut?"
Money seems like a god
to him.
It is more important
to him than I am,
that's for sure !

He Hits!

Battering Cycles

Your battering cycles became so evident after a while.
You lash out, you hit.
Then you become the puppy dog.
"I'm so sorry, honey. It won't ever happen again.
But you made me do it; you were disagreeing with me.
Please make love with me; make it all better again."
And so we do.
But this is like putting
a tiny bandage on a gaping wound.
And somehow I take responsibility
for patching up
the relationship once more.
But inside I cry
and plunge back into deep depression
and then denial--
and while I'm telling myself,
"Everything is wonderful,"
the pressure begins to build again--
back to the battering cycle!

Chapter 2

Jesus

Jesus

I had always assumed
that I was a Christian.
I loved going to church.
I prayed to Jesus,
but I had never heard Him speak to me.
       The year my son was in first grade,
       I car-pooled with a woman who said,
       "I'm a born-again Christian. What are you?"
       That started me thinking!
       She gave me biographies of Christians to read.
       I read about their faith,
       and I watched this new person in my life.
       Pat had a personal relationship with God
       and I wanted it.
A Father God who loved me?
That sounded too good to be true.
One day while she was visiting,
I asked her to pray with me
at my kitchen table.
I asked Jesus to forgive me
and enter into my life as Lord and Savior.
       February 9, 1977, in the midst
       of all my pain,
       my confusion,
       my loneliness,
       my lack of love,
       I met Jesus--
       really met Him--
       and that is when all the healing began.
       He is peace,
       He is a constant companion,
       He is Love . . .
       . . . and that is when all the healing began.

Chapter 3

Marriage

Part 2

My Husband Sleeps

It is night
outside and in my soul.
My husband sleeps,
but I, I am awake.
My head is pounding,
and my eyes are slits of pain.
The tears stream down my face.
I pace the floor
and stare up at the stars
shining through the windows of my house.
I drop to my knees
and bury my face in the chair--
silently sobbing,
as I cry again to God.
"Where is the solace
for my pain?
How long must I endure
this agony of anger,
of being beaten
for things I didn't do?"

My shoulders throb,
and in the other room,
my husband sleeps . . .

Setting Up

My artshows
are my world.
I am in control--
an established professional--
and Tim can't handle it.
He hates the crowds,
he hates the noise,
he hates the people.
He seems to hate that I'm
the center of attention.
(Or is it really
that he hates me?)
Yet--
somehow he insists upon
helping me set up,
but I am never fast enough
or organized enough for him.
He gets so angry
and he yells at me.
And I end up with my
traditional
stomach ache . . .
selling,
smiling at my customers,
making change,
pretending that
the tears
aren't
streaming
down
my face.
Pretending,
always
pretending . . .

A Place of Fire

O God,
I hate this place of fire,
of pain that overwhelms me.
It seems like almost every day
I'm in some sort of crisis
where I doubt that I can hang on
even another minute.
      Sometimes,
      it seems
      that no one can understand or share
      that screaming agony of pain
      that I'm in.
      I know all the right responses
      in my head,
      but my heart can't seem to get the message.
      It feels like
      I can't stand one more thing,
      or I will break.
      O God,
      You,
      only You,
      can change
      these circumstances of my life
      or change me to deal with it better.
      But is seems like I've been "dealing"
      with this pain forever--
      and the dealing never stops.
I need to rest
from this place of pain, Lord,
and I don't know where to turn.
O Lord, send Your warring angels,
for I need to rest from the battle
or I really will not make it
this time.

He Hits!

Giving It to God

My round blue living-room chair--
how many times
have I knelt
on the floor
and buried my head
in its softness,
muffling my screams
so only God can hear.

"Lord, I can't bear this any longer--
the intensity of anger,
and the hitting.
Will You keep Your promise,
that I must endure only so much
before You find an escape for me?"

I finally go to sleep,
feeling drained
but peaceful,
because I
gave it to my God.
And somehow when the new day breaks,
it is better
because I know He hears
and He has answered me.

Hawaii

Hawaii--
only our second vacation,
in eleven years of marriage.
I had so much anticipation--
so many longings for warmth and romance--
I couldn't believe we were really going!
Maybe,
away from the everyday hustle and bustle,
I would experience intimacy at last.
Instead, he invited another couple
so we were never alone.
I loved this couple
but I was trying desperately
to achieve closeness with Tim.
One night, in bed,
I mentioned my need
to be alone with him.
He was instantly angry--
I was questioning one of *his* decisions.
I got hit.
> Now when I think of Hawaii,
> I think of the awful contrast between
> my dreams
>> the color,
>> the beauty,
>> the warmth,
>> the perfume,
and what really happened there:
>> the cold,
>> black and white reality
>> of abuse.

Hawaii--
sort of spoiled
forever.

He Hits!

Unshed Tears

My heart is full
of sorrow,
of pain,
of unshed tears.
And, yet I know Your goodness, Lord,
Your mercies
that give me renewed energy
to go on.
I can praise You,
even in the midst of this,
because You never fail Your people
and I know that I know
that You won't fail me.

And the "forever waiting"
in *my* sight
is just a twinkling
in Your eye.

The Broken Door

You were livid.
I knew it this time
as, breathlessly, I ran
to our bedroom
and locked the door.
It was the farthest room away
from where you were.
I thought I was safe.
You might cool off.

I knew I was wrong
as I watched the lock shatter
and you break through
the ruined door.
My heart pounded
as you went for my throat.
Terror !
Choking!
I . . .
can't . . .
breathe . . . !

I thought I was safe,
but I was wrong.

He Hits!

The Circus

I just got back
from a three-day
artshow
and I have driven three hours
just
to get home.
Home . . . ahh!
I just want to rest,
to sleep.

Tim is taking the children
to the circus.
I don't even want to move,
but Tim insists
that I come with him.
So . . . I do.
But then
he is abusive
to everybody--
in a terrible mood--
yelling at poor little Janna
and totally extinguishing
her joy
in the circus.
Suddenly, from out of nowhere,
comes this clear inner vision--
of him
alone
without us.

Is this a premonition?
Tim--
who will you yell at then?

Free from the Destruction?

Tim, Tim,
my spirit cries over you.
My spirit cries over your bondages,
prisons learned in your past--
how you control people--
how you express anger and frustration.
I know that in our own strength,
we can never break these bondages
or set our own selves free from prison.

We've intertwined our lives,
for good or bad.
And this relationship
has been so fragile at times--
so broken.
Yet I appreciate your strengths,
your hard labor,
your many kindnesses to me . . .
especially in these last few months.
I do not reject you,
I forgive you.

I just wonder if the Lord isn't setting us
free from the destruction.

The Tiny Straw

It's kind of strange
how the abuse tapered off
in the last year.
It's almost like
Tim knew
that I was getting serious
about leaving.
In my prayers,
I had told the Lord,
"If there is one more time
of physical anger,
I
am
leaving."

It was in late summer,
just after we had celebrated
our fifteenth wedding anniversary.
Tim was putting some books
in his car trunk.
Jokingly, I referred to his "junk."
But this was a sensitive subject with him,
and he grabbed both my arms
and shook me hard.

Although it was a minor incident,
compared to the many
that had gone on before,
to my spirit,
it was the final,
tiny,
straw.

A Time of Mercy

O God,
get me out
of this mess I'm in--
this marriage that I stupidly got myself into
so many, so many years ago.

Get me out of this
in some creative way
that doesn't destroy
my two beautiful children--
that doesn't destroy
this man that I wed
for all the wrong reasons.

O God,
take me off this cross
that I have been hanging on
for all these many years.
Tell me that the years
of sacrifice are over
and that the time of mercy
has begun.

He Hits!

Chapter 4
Separation

I Take a Break

Separation.
A break--
I feel released from prison.
I . . .
can . . .
breathe!
But I feel scared.

What am I doing?
I am taking a break
to think,
to decide,
to see what God would have me do about my marriage.
Do I mean enough to Tim
for him to change?
For him to go to anger-management counseling
and finally deal with his own childhood--
with his own background of abuse?

I pray he will,
I watch
and wait . . .
. . . I take a break.

I Experienced Mercy

I experienced mercy.
Before my separation,
mercy was only a word to me--
not a living, breathing virtue.
I discovered freedom
to make choices
and I discovered
God's tender,
non-condemning love for me.
It was a special,
not-to-be missed
experience.
I didn't deserve it,
but
I
discovered
mercy.

Control!

Control!
You saw something in me.
I thought it was love,
and I was so hungry for love.
I used to ask you
what you loved about me.
You used to say
I was a good cook,
as if that was part of my character.
But it wasn't because of any qualities
I thought I had.
You sensed that I was someone
that you could control.
That's really the only reason
that you married me.

I'm only now getting in touch
with how angry I feel
as I see how
your desire to manipulate
permeates everyone you touch.

CONTROL!
I'm worth more than that.

Pain

Pain.
There's one thing about a painful experience:
it seems to sharpen my senses.
Once the initial experience has passed--
the rejection,
the agony,
the sting,
it brings, for me,
a heightened appreciation
of the people in the world
who reach out,
who are kind--
the true friends.
Sometimes I am glad
for that softening of heart
and the new awareness
that
pain
can
bring.

All I Do Is Sleep!

I'm so weary--
It has only been a few months
since my separation.
I want to bury my head
underneath my pillow
and just sleep.
Sleep, my body's reaction
to the stress.
I drag myself home from work
and make dinner
for the children,
clean up the kitchen,
and go to bed.
Janna and Andy
visit me there--
They take turns--
or sometimes all three of us
lie in my bed and talk.
I go to sleep early
but at 2 or 3 A.M.
my mind races--
I am awake--
worrying,
going over all the details
of my separation--
ants in the basement,
transmission problems,
bills to pay,
the kids' emotional survival,
divorce?--
wondering
what am I going to do now?
I'm so weary . . .

He Hits!

Road Signs Along the Way

Agony.
The agony of deciding what I should do.

Should I get a legal separation?
Should I divorce?
I am a Christian, and Christians don't divorce.
Would it be sin?

But little clues seem to point the way.
If Tim could only show me
that I mean something to him
other than caretaker or cook or washer.
If he could only show true sorrow, true repentance
for all the wounds,
for all the pain,
I might go back.
But he calls to ask about a stain on his floor;
he comes over angry at Janna
and throws papers in her face . . .

These little road signs along the way
seem to point the way,
and little by little,
I am deciding.

Decisions

Decisions--
I'm making decisions
with a vengeance!

I move my business
out of my house
into a retail location.
I decide to separate from Tim.
I find a duplex
for me and the children.
I pack and move out of our house--
the only home the children have known.
New bank accounts--checking and savings--
I even order garbage pick-up
and refinish a piece of furniture.

At first,
it was exhilarating--
just having freedom
to make my own decisions
(probably for the first time in my life).
But now,
it has become exhausting
as I reel under
the trauma
from all the changes.

Decisions and consequences--
I am exhausted!

He Hits!

Holidays

Holidays--
there's another one coming up.
Close by, it's sneaking up on me.

Aloneness.
Shared custody!
A lot of holidays fall on weekends,
when the children
have to visit their father,
and I'm alone.
Even though people ask me to share with them,
somehow
it's not the same.
No anticipation,
of cooking the meal,
of celebration.
No family . . .
It's not the same.
And people talk about holidays so much.
"How was your day?" they ask.
I wish they wouldn't ask.
It was just a day
that somehow I got through.

It's not the same.

Is This the Last Day, Lord?

Is this the last day, Lord?
I want to know Your will.
I want to joyfully anticipate
the blessings You have in store for me,
because I have already experienced
so much of the pain, Lord.
Is it Your will to set me free?
O God, my God,
forsake me not.
Hear my cry, Lord.
Hear the deepest longings
of my heart--
know when I pray in the Spirit, Lord,
when only You can understand,
I pour out my heart to You
for only You can untangle
the chains of my circumstances
and set me free.

I wait upon You, O Lord,
and even in the waiting,
You have renewed my strength.

He Hits!

Like a Crutch

Sometimes,
I think
I used God like a crutch,
falsely hearing Him make my decisions
because I was too afraid
to make my own--
or too afraid to deal with the consequences
my choices would create.
Instead, I stayed for years--
too long--
in an unhealthy situation,
sure that God was denying me the choice to leave.
Now, I see
the Hawaii trip
in a whole new light.
I cried and prayed all that night after being hit.
It was a turning point in my marriage.
I visualized catching the morning plane
and heading straight for the attorney's office
and divorce.
But, as I prayed, I thought I heard God say "No!"
Suddenly it was His responsibility
and I didn't have to make a choice,
not yet.
Sometimes, I think I used Him like a crutch!

Transfer

Janna,
my daughter,
I can't bear
the pain of knowing
that now your dad is hitting you.
I can't stand it!
I feel guilty
because I'm not there,
acting as the buffer zone.
I feel guilty
because now it's you
and not me.
But I feel vindicated, in a way,
that I did the right thing
to take us all out of there.
We'll find healing yet . . .
I promise you.
We'll love each other,
you and I,
and we'll be whole.

Chapter 5

Submission, the Church and Abuse

Submission

I used to believe that biblical submission
meant meekly accepting whatever action
my husband decided to take.
Or that maybe my hellish situation
was my chastisement from the Lord.
Yes, I was the martyr--
or a rug, and Tim could wipe his feet on me.

But as I grow to understand the Scriptures,
I can see how wrong I was.
That beautiful example--
that husbands must love their wives
as Christ loves His church--
means that if the wife must be
in submission to her husband,
then the husband must be in submission to God.
Otherwise it never works.

It takes two
to make this confusing subject of submission
even understandable.
It takes two.

No--
it takes three.

A Guilt Trip

For a while
I attended two churches at the same time--
one, the denominational church of my childhood;
the other, a fundamental, evangelical church.
Because the second one was so small,
I thought I formed a love-bond with those people.
I know I loved them.
Everything was wonderful . . .
until my separation
and thoughts about divorce.
To them,
divorce,
for any reason,
was sin.
The pastor and his wife told me that if I divorced,
I could not fellowship with "the body."
I would be a stumbling block--a bad example--
and I could not minister to anyone.
(But the pastor's wife told me privately
that I could stay separated until
Tim committed adultery--
then it would be *his* sin, and I would be "free!")
      I could not believe their legalism!
      I could not allow them to control my life.
      They were playing God!
      I had to leave,
      but I felt so sad.
      Now, I'm dead to those people--
      a whole church.
      They don't see me or speak to me .
      Isn't it sad what we do to each other
      sometimes
      in the name of religion?
      Guilt--the gift that keeps on giving . . .

Hug, Hug

Fundamental,
evangelical churches!
Will I ever hear the name without going insane?
They say they "love you, love you,"
hug, hug . . .
But then they
poke
and pry
and judge
until I think it must be me
who doesn't measure up!
Not quite,
oh, no.

Another meeting?
Wednesday, Friday, and all day Sunday
(just another hour or two),
and in between we can clean the church or paint
or I can calligraphy some Scripture verses on the side--
for free, of course.

All for God?
Yes, all for God--
as if we had to win His favor
or His love.
All for God, hug, hug. Oh yes, Amen!

More Guilt

I remember sitting in the "Christian" counselor's office.
She said, "I can see that you're angry!"
(like that was some big sin).
I remember feeling guilty,
the way she accused me of an honest emotion.

After I left there, I thought,
Angry? Of course, I'm angry!
I'm not a perfect person,
but I've done my best to be a good wife,
a helpmate,
and I've been beaten up for fifteen years.

I spent so many years
with so little feeling--
so much repression and denial.
I'd suppressed that emotion of anger for all those years
and I'm finally feeling rage
at being manipulated this way--
by Tim and now by the counselor!

Angry? Of course I'm angry!

And to Mary (a "Christian" Counselor)

So . . . you said you could live with a gorilla--
good for you!--
because your trust lies in God.
Well, mine does too.
Because without Him and His healing I know
I would not be as whole
and sane as I am now.
Woman, don't you ever read anything?
About abuse?
About learned helplessness
and passivity
and beating
and anger and fear
and sick dependency?
Just like the rotten apple in the barrel--
it makes everyone sick.
But you have made a god of marriage
when you put the value of the institution
before the sanctity of human life.
And piously
say that you would have to
answer to God for advising
anyone to leave a marriage.
Well, lady, you've got that right!
And I'm in danger of judging you
for your poor counsel,
for piling on the guilt some more.
I can only pray that you will read and learn
before more damage is done
to someone else in similar circumstances.
Here--you can have
my gorilla!

He Hits!

Statistics

Statistics show that more Christian women
stay in abusive homes
than non-Christian women.
And if I'd listened
to that "Christian" counselor
or to that little church,
I would have been manipulated once again,
being told what to think,
what to feel,
what to do.
I agree with their view--
the Bible's view--
that physical adultery
is wrong, is sin.
But I disagree with their view
which denies that physical abuse
is a form of spiritual adultery,
which argues that it doesn't
somehow
break the marriage bond.
God says
there are consequences
for our actions,
even if the little church
and that crazy "counselor"
disagree.
And I can't accept
the abuse continuing
generation
after
generation.
Statistics--
I didn't want to be
another statistic!

A Special Bonus

When I was first a Christian,
I used to think with joy,
that it was a special bonus
to have an instant, loving family
of brothers and sisters
who immediately accepted me
because I was one of God's family.
But there are so few love-givers,
and, oh, so many more
who judge and seem to pile on guilt.

They weigh each situation
according to their own morality,
which often has little to do with Jesus.

Have mercy!
Walk a mile in my shoes
before you comment on how I choose
to live my life,
before you point out all the many specks in my eye
while the log is sticking out a mile
from yours!

He Hits!

I Have to Please

Isn't it ironic how, for so many years,
I went around from counselor to counselor,
like a squirrel in a cage,
as I begged them to help me cope?
To women, to men,
and the Domestic Violence unit at the "Y," I cried:
"Help me endure life with this angry person!
Help me save my marriage!
Change me--or make him stop!"
But the beatings and the anger lingered on.
> It gave me a sense of purpose,
> such a feeling of virtue,
> to keep my marriage together
> when all the world was losing theirs.

And then the years of beatings took their toll
on any love I might have felt
or any covenant there might have been.
"Enough of this," I said.
"It's over."
> But then the trouble started--
> the judgments, the advice,
> the guilt from people I love
> and who, I thought, loved me.
> I was a Christian;
> I could not leave my marriage.
> Sin, it would be sin.
> Unforgivable, unpardonable.
> Suddenly, to them, I was "rebellious."
> Me, rebellious?
> After fifteen years of living with that anger?

I finally learned the irony
of trying desperately to please
all those other people
when it is only God I have to please.

Chapter 6

Divorce

In the Heart

Divorce in the heart.
I wonder when
that really happened?

When did I hit that turning point
from caring
to contempt?
From respect
to revulsion?
When did making love
turn into just sex?
And sacrament
into sacrilege?
When did I finally
take my wedding picture
off the wall
because it mocked me?
The promise of love
in that celebration
was fulfilled only
in remembered misery.
Only God can know
that the final decree
had already happened
in my heart.

I'm Losing

Today
I'm in pain
in the pit of my stomach.
It makes me depressed
to know that I put up with all that abuse
for so many years
and now I am losing everything!

    The house,
    economic security . . .
    I'm broke
    and the money isn't stretching
    to pay for counselors,
    to pay for attorneys.
    I HATE fighting,
    but I have to be strong.
    I hate it.

I feel like I'm losing,
losing,
losing.
I hate this.

My Weakest Point

Sometimes
I feel like
I'm at the weakest
emotional point
of my whole life--
broken, sad, discouraged.
I'm watching all my dreams
shatter,
as if it were my heart
that is breaking.
I want to say,
"Take it all--
all our material possessions."
It would be so much easier!
I don't want to fight
with Tim--
but this is the whole future
of my children
that I'm fighting for.
Why should they have to suffer
financially--
along with
all the emotional pain
that they are going through?
I feel so weak,
but I must be strong.
O God,
help me to be strong . . .
and fair.

You Did It All

Poor Tim.
Isn't it ironic
how you never had a repairman
or anyone do anything for you
that you could do yourself?
You saved so much money
not going on vacations
and you kept so busy
building and fixing
that we couldn't ever play
or go to a movie.
Not to mention going to a motel
for the weekend.
Isn't it ironic how
you saved so much money
only to give half of it to me
during the divorce?
Now I have to pay a repairman
and a builder
when we could have done things together.
Isn't it a shame!

Just Goodbye

I say, GOODBYE.
I have to say goodbye to family-ness,
to togetherness,
to holding hands and making love.
Goodbye to dreams of being old together
and watching grandchildren play.
Goodbye to the house I helped build and decorate--
to the many yards of concrete I troweled.
Goodbye to apple trees and the flowering cherry
and springtime with wild flowers in profusion.
Goodbye to entertaining other couples.
    And goodbye to all the negatives!
    Goodbye to all the junk you collected--
    three extra buildings of pack-rat material
    (and even that wasn't enough).
    Goodbye to never being able
    to open the bedroom window.
    Goodbye to freezing in the winter
    and broiling in the summer
    because you wouldn't let me use
    the heat or the air-conditioning!
    GOODBYE TO CANNING!
    Goodbye to dirty jokes
    and your strange sense of humor.
    Goodbye to being a slave to your eating patterns.
    Goodbye to being a slave, period.
    Goodbye to being beaten, choked,
    kicked, and constantly put down.
    Goodbye to never being appreciated
    as a person, Christian, or artist.
    Goodbye to laying out your clothes.
    Goodbye to stinginess.
    Goodbye to paranoia--yours!
Just goodbye.

Peace--at Any Price

Yes, I know
that the destructive patterns
of our relationship
were my fault too.

I was too passive--
too submissive.
I wanted peace at any price--
to avoid conflict
if at all possible.

Maybe if I had taken a stand
in the beginning--
while there was still love--
I could have saved our marriage.

Every story has two sides--
I wanted peace
at any price--
I paid the price!

Boy Vs Girl?

Isn't it strange
that Tim
never ever hit our son?
Andy hasn't even witnessed
any physical abuse.
In fact, it was hard
for him even to accept
the reality
of my report that his dad
hit me and Janna,
and to accept
the reality
of the subsequent divorce.
But Janna has no doubts!
I think back to the time
when Tim hit me
in the stomach
when I was pregnant
with our daughter.
Isn't it strange,
it was Janna
instead of Andy
inside me?
Did Tim sense
the baby was a girl
even then?

Do You Have to Choose?

Goodbye, dear friends.
I guess it was an illusion
that I could keep your friendship and your love.
I guess it is hard on friends--
having to decide
who is
the "good" or "bad" person.
But does there have to be a side to choose?
       I don't say "goodbye" lightly--
       it's as if my already lacerated heart
       is being torn apart once more.
       I didn't think I could bear it, but I guess I can.
       I just wonder if you think I'm lying--
       lying after all this time!
       Or if you just can't handle that ugly little word--
       ABUSE--
       that couldn't happen in the nicest homes!
It doesn't seem to matter
that I've never said
anything mean or bitter about him.
It doesn't seem to matter that I've tried to be decent.
Or never told you details that would curl your hair.
It doesn't seem to matter when I'm lonely.
At Christmas time I got your card with "best wishes"
instead of "love."
       If I have to have an amputation,
       I would just as soon get it over with
       instead of by degrees.
       And so I'll say,
       "Goodbye."

He Hits!

Why Did I Stay So Long?

Why did I stay so long?
In the beginning,
I suppose,
my low self-esteem
made me stay.
I always thought
that things would get better
or that I could do something
to prevent his anger.
And as a Christian,
I believed in my commitment
to the marriage--
to the children--
until it became obvious
(even to me)
that my spirit was almost dead,
so depressed that I could hardly respond to anything.
And the children were being affected
by example
(if nothing else).
It's hard to leave,
because the known pain
seems less scary
than the unknown.
It's hard to know when the time is right.
Why did I wait so long . . . ?
For all these reasons--
but
who
ever
really knows?

Self-Esteem

I know it is only because of God
that I have any
self-esteem at all.
Growing up,
I felt that
my parents approved of me
only when I was a size ten,
with clear complexion,
short hair,
wearing the very best clothes,
and getting "A " grades in school.
Everything seemed so conditional.
I felt unloved
and unworthy in every way
because I felt like I didn't measure up.
And then Tim
just reinforced
all those opinions I had of myself.
He never seemed to think
I had it all together
as a wife, either.
But then I met Jesus
and He began my healing--
letting me know
that I am, first of all,
a child of God,
created in His image,
known to Him even before my conception.
He loves me
and will never leave me
and that gives me
my self-esteem!

He Hits!

The Scarlet "D"

Sometimes I feel like I have
The Scarlet "D"
tattooed on my forehead--
blinking, flashing.
I just hate being divorced.
There is something so comforting,
so secure
in being married!
But the reality
of my marriage
was a far cry
from my "idea" of marriage.
I never once thought about divorce
in those early years.
Even with all the awful stuff going on,
divorce was never an option for me.
But I used to have these detailed
daydreams . . .
planning what I would do if he would die.

I escaped inside my head.

Isn't it strange
how my commitment to marriage was so strong
that I could contemplate
Death
before Divorce?
Sometimes I'm sure
I have that
Scarlet "D"
blazing on my forehead.

I'm Sorry

And do you know I'm sorry?
I went through a loving time
          a serving time
          a hoping time
          a dying time
          a martyr time
          a hating time
          a crying time
          an angry time.
But now I just feel sorry
that I couldn't do my part
to stop violence between people
and in relationships,
to stop destruction
in families
and in the world.
And do you know I
just
feel
sorry?

He Hits!

I Forget

After I'm away from pain for a while
I forget what it is like.
Sort of like a woman giving birth--
After the baby is born,
she can't remember the labor.
So now, three years after my separation,
I can forget the pain . . .
I can forgive,
but I don't know if I did the right thing.
Sometimes, I think about suffering--
how a person in a wheelchair,
or with a disease,
can't just walk away from pain.
That's what I did--
I walked away from suffering.
And I don't know if I did the right thing
or not.
I forgot the pain.

Lord,
help me not to forget
all
the
pain.

Divorce

DIVORCE
pain
death
separation
suffering--
I know why God
hates divorce:
EVERYONE loses.
But in the midst
of intense
heart-pain,
I feel alive
FREE--
soaring like
a butterfly.

He Hits!

Chapter 7

Reaching Out

Prepared to Reach Out

O Lord,
sometimes I chafe,
sometimes I resist Your voice.
I resent all the times I think
You're talking just to me.
Why do I always have to change?
Why is it always me?
But, then, I know, Lord,
that because of Your voice,
because of Your discipline,
because of Your chastening,
I am different.
I am more compassionate,
I am more loving,
and because of these dealings,
I can reach out to others
and love them
with
Your
love!

To Vicky

To Vicky (who works near me):
As I was leaving work tonight
I saw you being pushed around
in the parking lot.
(Even the place was an invasion of your privacy.)
I saw you wring your hands through your hair
in stress and in despair.
I cried for you
and I cried for me
as I remembered the countless times
that I endured the same kind of treatment.
And the pain I feel for you is so intense,
it physically hurts.
Because I know if you take a little
of this kind of abuse,
it only gets worse and worse.
And if you are like I was,
you'll make the mistake of thinking
that it won't happen again.
Can I help you?
Will you listen?
Or could you just use my shoulder
to cry on?

Abuse
(To a Man I Met Who Was Battering His Wife)

No one ever deserves it,
no matter what they have said
or done,
or not done or not said.
We always have lots of business stress
and working pressure to make ends meet,
but can that ever justify
expressions of violence toward another?
What motivation would we have
for working--
without that special someone to share it with
or someone to come home to?
Life would be just
loneliness . . .
depression . . .
and work would seem like dust and ashes
in your mouth.
We need to cherish and nurture each other
as though we are fragile flowers.
Buying flowers can never be
the only expression of love.
Because flowers
and kisses
can never undo the DAMAGE
that abuse causes to our own self-respect
or to our respect for the other person.
And when respect dies,
love dies too.
Each instance of emotional or physical abuse
is like a speeding train
heading for the station of divorce,
and only we can stop
that train from going any farther.

He Hits!

New Life

I hear that there's a new woman--
a new victim--
in Tim's life.
I hear that she is
a care giver,
warm and loving
(his favorite kind),
and she has money too!
>Do I have a responsibility
>to tell her about
>his abuse?
>I write this story so that no one
>will have to go through
>this again--
>would she listen?
>Would I have listened
>if someone had
>tried
>to
>tell
>me?
Maybe she will be able to read this
before it's too late
or maybe God
can take away Tim's battering
and they will be all right.
I hope so.
I pray so.
I'm not supposed to know about her--
he makes Janna promise not to tell--
but everyone else seems to know
and I hear anyway--
there's a new woman
in his life.

Chapter 8

Healing

True Friends

Friends are good, Lord.
Thank You so much for friends.

Thank You for friends
who stick by me,
even in the bad times
when sometimes they don't
understand--
or even know about the abuse.

Thank You for friends
who somehow can remain friends
with both of us--
who don't choose sides.
I feel blessed.

Thank You for friends--
for loving people who reach out,
who care.
Especially after so much
judgment
and condemnation,
it is like
refreshing rain
after a drought.

I feel nourished . . .

Thank You, Lord, for friends.

Why Can't We Be Like Karen?

I remember one hot day,
on the way to Bible study,
I met a woman named Karen.
That very first day
she stayed for lunch at my house.
She skipped the ordinary chit chat
and instead became immediately vulnerable to me,
sharing the secrets of her heart--
her pain.
I, in turn,
could bear to tell her
that my husband was abusing me.
     From that day on,
     Karen phoned me
     every day.
     She prayed with me,
     she cared for me.
     I trusted people so little
     at that point,
     that sometimes I wondered
     if she was for real.
     And my mistrust hurt her feelings.
     Little by little,
     her love penetrated my very being.
     I'm sure God knew
     that it would take
     a human-person--
     a special Karen--
     to teach me how
     to trust,
     to heal,
     to love again.
Oh, thank You, God,
for sending Karen!

He Hits!

Questions????

Sometimes
I ask myself questions.

> How did I get into that mess anyway?
> How did I end up marrying that person?
> Was I so lonely,
> so starved for love,
> that I would marry anyone who asked?
> Did I think that
> any marriage
> was better than
> no marriage at all?
> Or was my self-esteem so low
> that I didn't think much of myself
> or recognize an angry person?
> Was I so used to following orders as a child,
> that I fit right into Tim's mold for me?

I can't always understand
and yet I know--
yes, I know--
that my life is forever changed
because of this experience,
and I believe that God can bring good
out of any circumstances . . .
. . . I know He has brought good to me.

Who I Am

When I tell my story,
I do so for my own healing--
to say,
"This is who I am
and what I've been through.
Can it help anyone out there?"
I don't re-live my experiences to discredit him
but, rather, to make more people aware
of the commonality
of violence and abuse
right in our own neighborhoods
today.
And I do so for our healing,
to help say,
"This must stop!
We must learn to treat
each other with respect
and with love!"
We
must
stop!

                    He Hits!

Delayed Reactions

I shocked everyone
when I moved out.
I had kept silent for so long
that very few people knew
the real circumstances.
And even when people asked,
I could not speak.
Now,
now as the healing has begun,
I want to speak,
to tell my story,
to get it out.
(It's like the men who live through war--
they have delayed reactions,
and so do I.)
Now,
now I want to speak
but no one
asks
anymore . . .

An Ode to Green Beans

Green beans, green beans.
I picked you,
I snapped you,
I cut you and canned you.
I dreamed you
in nightmares
marching by
in little green rows.
It was not a love affair we had,
green beans.
Now I'm free forever
from the quota I had
every summer.
I'm sure the grocery store
can do just as well
canning--
green beans.

Sister-in-Law

Sister-in-law,
I miss you.
We had a comfortable,
warm relationship.
I was aunt
to your children
and friend
to you.
Now,
everything has changed!
You are pleasant
when we see
each other,
but there is distance
and pain
between us.
I used to be related,
and now it seems
strange and sad
to be nothing--

Sister-in-law,
I miss you.

Garbage!

In my new life
I don't take
even the smallest freedoms
for granted.
I feel excited
every time
the garbage
gets picked up.

> Tim even controlled the trash!
> We stored it
> in fifty-gallon drums
> and he, then, hauled it
> to the refuse landfill site
> every three months
> (whether we needed it or not!).
> *We saved money!*
> Sometimes I can't believe
> that I gave up
> so much personal freedom.

Every week,
I am thrilled
and grateful
when the garbage gets picked up!

He Hits!

The Uncoupling Process

It's such a strange thing
going through the uncoupling process--
I believe that marriage
should combine physical, emotional, and spiritual
intimacy.
Even though Tim and I only seemed to share
physical oneness,
still, it takes time
going from being "one" to two again.
>We lived separate lives
>in separate places,
>but
>my thinking was still dominated
>by that strong, forceful personality
>which I had allowed to control me for so long.
>We had a co-dependency.
>I remember walking down the grocery aisle
>and seeing food he used to like--
>I'd wonder if he was eating right,
>but then I would remember
>that I was not responsible for feeding him
>anymore.
>Or I would hear a joke he would enjoy.
>And when I bought my car,
>I looked only at models he used to like.
>I wouldn't do that now, but at first,
>I was still thinking and living as part of him.
My thoughts are becoming independent
as I work toward healing and wholeness.
It takes time--
some growing time--
through the uncoupling process.

Hungry for Love

Starved, starved,
you'd think I was starved,
or so thirsty
that I had never seen water.
But You, O Lord, are the source
of all living water.
Haven't I yet learned
that "my heart is hungry
until it rests
in Thee"?
O Lord,
be the source
for me
of my love,
of the love
that satisfies my spirit--
that satisfies the yearning in me
to be loved--
and to love.

He Hits!

Roses and Respect

Cherish me . . .
"Cherish"--
such a wonderfully old-fashioned word.
I want to be cherished,
cuddled,
showered with
roses and respect.
Given to,
because I'm a giver.
I want to give--
but never be a doormat again--
to outpour all the love
in my overflowing heart--
I want to cherish you
but only if
you'll
cherish me.

Speeding

Sometimes when I'm riding in a car,
I have a flashback to those many times
I was a passenger
with Tim driving angrily and going at least 65 mph
on city streets,
taking the corners on two wheels
as I was screaming,
"Stop and let me out!"
But he never did.
And I was too chicken to jump.
I was a captive,
and he picked
the time
and place
to explode
at me.
Sometimes I have a flashback
and experience that momentary terror,
but then I remember:
It's over now.
I don't ride in that car anymore!

He Hits!

I Am Happy

Happy.
I'm so happy!
Who would have thought
how contented I'd be--
alone--
alone with all the
responsibilities
of providing for my little family?
Alone, but not lonely.
I feel like a kid
at a birthday party
or on Christmas morning--
gazing with awe
at the colored lights,
awaiting with excitement
what life and
God
have in store
for me.

Content

Content!
It feels so good to be content.
It's quiet here in my little house,
so peaceful.
But I remember that first weekend
when my children left for their weekly visit
with their dad.
I felt so much anxiety
and stress.
I had gone from child,
to student,
to wife,
to mother,
and I'd never lived alone.
I remember that first weekend,
I didn't know if I could bear
those hours stretched before me.
Alone--
a scary word.
But, now, I thank You, Lord,
for those very, scary, painful times
when I was forced to be alone,
to think,
to pray,
to grow content!

He Hits!

God Can Turn Tears into Dancing

One Sunday in church,
we sang a song:
"You have turned
my tears into dancing."
And I thought,
"How true that is
in my life."
I used to cry,
and now I'm dancing--
almost every day--
truly a miracle!
I'm so happy
to be dancing . . .

To Laugh Again

I have a sense of humor,
I really do.
But it was buried
under layers
upon layers
of pain.
Now, in the healing process,
my sense of humor
is beginning to
peep out--
bubbling over in unexpected ways--
I love to laugh!
I find the funny side
in unexpected situations--
I'm so glad that
my sense of humor
didn't die forever.
Oh, thank You, Lord,
for bringing back the laughter.
I love to laugh!

He Hits!

A Day Like This

A day like this.
I give thanks
for a day like this.

    Everyone
    in my little family
    is happy with each other--
    welcoming,
    loving.
    Andy has been gone for four days
    and we are so glad
    to have him back.
    We know the time
    is short
    until he leaves for college.
    My heart overflows
    with joy
    as we share
    love and laughter.
    I am totally content . . .

I give thanks
for a day like this.

I Turn Up My Face

Dear Father God,
I feel like a sunflower,
with my little face turned up
trustingly,
confidently,
receiving Your blessings,
basking in the sunlight of Your love
for me,
just for me.
I used to be in such a dark,
cold, place,
suffering, waiting.
Now my time has come,
and the sunshine feels so warm
upon my face.
The rays reach down,
clear down,
to heal and warm
all those bruised places inside me.
And Your Sonshine, Lord,
feels so warm upon my face.

You Will Restore

*"And I will restore to you
the years that the locust hath eaten,
the cankerworm, and the palmerworm,
my great army which I sent among you."*

This is the verse
that jumped out at me,
way back,
when I was praying about
my separation.
God quickened it to my spirit--
and He has brought it to pass--
the renewing of all those lost years--
a chance
to
begin
again . . .

Restoration

My heart is so full, Lord,
of love,
of life,
of laughter--
I've been released from prison!
And every day
just keeps getting better and better!
Out of the fullness of my heart
I thank You, Lord,
for renewing and restoring the years
the locust has eaten . . .
The work is never done, but . . .
You have restored!

My Gift to You

And if God
can restore
me . . .
He can
restore
you, too!

Bibliography

Dobson, James. *Love Must Be Tough* (Waco, Texas: Word Books, 1983).

Green, Holly Wagner. *Turning Fear to Hope* (Nashville, Tennessee: Thomas Nelson Publishers, 1984).

Hirschmann, Maria Anne. *Please Don't Shoot, I'm Already Wounded* (Wheaton, Illinois: Tyndale House, 1979).

Lovett, C.S. *The Compassionate Side of Divorce* (Baldwin Park, California: Personal Christianity, 1978).

Nicarthy, Ginny. *Getting Free* (Seattle, Washington: The Seal Press).

Olson, Esther Lee and Kenneth Taylor. *No Place to Hide* (Wheaton, Illinois: Tyndale House, 1979).

Savina, Lydia. *Help for the Battered Woman* (South Plainfield, New Jersey: Bridge Publishing, Inc. 1987).

Strom, Kay Marshall. *In the Name of Submission* (Portland, Oregon: Multnomah Press, 1986).

Walker, Lenore. *The Battered Woman* (New York: Harper and Row, 1979).

For a free catalog of other personal testimonies
helpful to hurting women
(about divorce, breast cancer, addictions, overweight,
rape, handicaps, illness and/or death of a child . . .),
send a stamped, self-addressed envelope to

Star Books, Inc.
408 Pearson Street
Wilson, NC 27893

(919) 237-1591